Safe Haven

Beautiful Helen
with all my
love
Mandy
pet

Mandy Imlay

Grosvenor House
Publishing Limited

This book is published by
Grosvenor House Publishing Ltd
Link House
140 The Broadway, Tolworth, Surrey, KT6 7HT.
www.grosvenorhousepublishing.co.uk

This book is a work of fiction. Any resemblance to
people or events, past or present, is purely coincidental.

A CIP record for this book
is available from the British Library

ISBN 978-1-78623-139-0

DEDICATION

I want to dedicate this book to the real author, the Holy Spirit, who has guided me through the rough seas of life bringing me to land safely in the arms of our Heavenly Father and Jesus, His Son.

I also dedicate this book to the love of my life, Andrew.

You have loved me through some very challenging times and it is a testament to your love that we are still together and looking forward to the best season of our lives so far.

I want to thank my father and step-mother, my five lovely brothers and their families and my two beautiful step sisters for loving me despite our differences. I feel very privileged to be part of such a special family.

I also want to thank the wonderful woman who introduced me to the Holy Spirit and the book of Song of Songs. She is the one the Lord chose to nurture and mentor me, to encourage me and love me even in my weakness. You, Jewel Simpson, modelled the whole ethos of Song of Songs for me, your deep humility and love brings tears to my eyes. You truly are the Lord's Precious Jewel and your name appears constantly in His Book of Remembrance.

You even gave me the name and artwork for this book. A day or so before I was commissioned to write, the Lord prompted you to send me this beautiful painting, Safe Haven. I had already written the poem, The Harbour, and many of the poems that appear in the book itself.

He told me to write this book in six days and then to take a Sabbath Rest. It was so easy, such a download, no striving, no effort! Such is a life lived in the Spirit!

Now I have completed this book, I have crossed over into the life of the Spirit, and my life will never be the same again. This Rose is about to blossom into the full destiny, written inside her while she was still in the womb.

A destiny written in heaven before the foundations of the world, a tiny part of the Body of Christ, joining together with its many differing parts to become the whole.

Lord Jesus come and take your place as our Head

Lord Jesus return once more to this earth and make our reconciliation complete.

CONTENTS

INTRODUCTION

This book tells the story of one woman's journey out of the rough seas of religion and back into the Harbour of Love, the Safe Haven of the Spirit of Truth. It is a work of fiction, loosely based on my life. I am part of the church and I love the church but there have been times in the past where I have been alienated from certain parts of the Body of Christ due to misunderstanding and hurt. This is the story of The Creator's Love transforming a broken heart and bringing deep healing and reconciliation.

THE HARBOUR

Boats a bobbing on the sea
The harbour is groaning with its fare
Boats bringing people
Boats bringing food
Boats from everywhere.

With the sun, the people emerge
With the storm, they disappear
Such is the destiny of our seaside town
Our refuge by the sea.

Salt slashes the pavements
The paint is dulled and chipped
The walls coloured in every hue
Pink, blues, yellows and whites
The paint dissolves as winter takes hold
The café doors are closed
Hibernation begins.
It is time to take stock
It is time to rest and redecorate
It is time to sleep.

The spring comes, the flowers begin to appear
The doors are opened to air the newly painted homes.
Homes repaired and renewed
Homes waiting to embrace their visitors
Those waiting to flock to these shores again.

The harbour opens up its arms
Spreading ever wider to embrace all who come
No one will be turned away from these shores
For the harbour belongs to the Great Shepherd
The Great Lighthouse who guides us on our way
The Safe Haven leading to our destiny.

CHAPTER 1

THE HAMSTER WHEEL

The journey begins as I step off the hamster's wheel of busyness. The clouds engulf me in a wave of fear and yet I see my foot take a step off, it seems as if I have no control and my foot is walking off all by itself. I see myself follow my foot and I hear the voice again.

"Come, Beloved, come away with Me."

I have no idea where I am going, but I am drawn to this voice, this voice which whispers to me, this voice which woos me and loves me just as I am.

"Don't look back, My love, look forward for We have so much to show you".

I begin to follow this voice, the whisper stretching out from my ear and forming itself into an outline, an outline of I know not what, but an outline just the same.

The figure begins to dance His way forward, skipping up the mountains and hills that materialise out of nowhere.

A song begins to invade my senses, a deep throbbing down in the base of my belly, the beat drums rhythmically tapping ever so gently at my womb. A door is opening inside me, a door to a new life, a new way. I am clothed in the most beautiful aroma that I have ever smelled. This perfume must be bottled, I think, it will make a fortune. My senses are on fire, I feel intoxicated, drunk in the spiralling hues of the rainbow that shoot out and assault me at every turn.

Where is this mysterious figure, where has He gone? I look around me, I look out into the distance and there I can just make out a yellow door in a red brick wall.

"It is our secret garden," I hear, "our garden of love."

I am amazed, utterly astounded.

"He's lying, you can't go in there, you are not good enough. Look at the state of you, what were you thinking?"

I am confused, this voice is not the soothing loving voice I followed here. I look around, but I see nothing. I shiver as a sudden chill comes over me. I look down at my torn dress, the holes in my shoes, I see the dirt embedded deep under my finger nails, the scars where I have cut into my skin.

I am spiralling back into my past, back into the madness, back into the darkness, the pit of putrid hopelessness.

I am hungry, so very hungry, I cry out wanting my mother, but I am left rocking back and forth, back and forth. I feel so sick and yet the rocking goes on and on, the laughter in the distance getting louder and louder, the stale urine the only warmth I am to experience.

The pungent smell assails me and I am back in the darkness, surrounded by rich pickings and yet this royal babe is left unattended, robbed of love, robbed of life.

The cry inside me begins to change, the scream of desperation takes over, everything goes black.

I am falling, down and down, round and round. Fear creeps up and latches onto my heart and tugs it further down, spiralling, spiralling, out of control. Icy fingers reach out to touch me, my flesh crawls and I cry out once more for help, there must be someone out there, someone who can help the helpless.

A wind of change is blown in with the warmth of summer. There is a fragrance of roses lingering in the air, the night is turning into day as the sun rises in the blue sky. The morning is dressed in the colour of pink pastels, the wash of blue, bathing in the light of the sun, melting under the soft glow of the golden light. The dazzling brightness of the dawn starts to push through, the darkness is forgotten as the light enfolds this royal babe in its arms.

The birds announce their arrival in the sweetest melody that I have ever heard. Their song soars through the air and lands gently on my cheek, caressing me and awakening the breath inside me.

I feel a kiss blow into my mouth, a warm arm enfolds me, a royal breast finds its way ever so gently into my mouth. I begin to suck greedily, gulping as the colostrum fills my stomach and the royal protection is installed.

I am washed ever so gently and swaddled and held. I hear the lullaby lilt its way over me, it feels like liquid love, a warm glow filling me from inside out.

I am tugged back into the present once more, I begin to look for the wheel, the world's wheel, the busy round-about of sameness dressed up as church. But it is not there, I can't find it. Panic sets in, where am I? Where am I going?

"To the promised land." I hear as He laughs out loud.

CHAPTER 2
THE SECRET GARDEN

I am standing in front of the little yellow door. There is light flowing out from underneath and I can smell the beautiful perfume again, carried on the breeze. The singing has begun, this exquisite song calling me to come inside. Tentatively, I reach out for the green knocker and begin to turn it.

"You might need this," the voice is gentle but I am frightened and need a moment to calm myself again. I turn around and there lying in the grass is a key. I pick it up and put it into the lock. As I turn the key, the door begins to open all by itself, the knocker has turned into a red beating heart. As I walk inside I am surrounded by the welcome committee, robins dancing joyously round and round me, their red breasts puffing out in a mysterious beat that mesmerises me and draws me further in.

I seem to be in a beautiful garden and as I look, I begin to see that it is in four distinct sections. The first section is a rose garden, carefully cultivated and cared for. There is a gardener in the distance pruning and watering the many varieties and colours on show. I see a little white gate and walk through into the next section. I seem to be in a field with its emerald green grass gently rolling down the hill towards a river. Close to the water's edge is a tall apple tree bending over with the weight of its fruit.

I look over to the other side of the river and here I see the river move out into a cascading waterfall of colours. This rainbow waterfall seems to flow out from heaven itself, its power pronounced, the thunder deafening.

"Come, let Me take you to the last part of this garden."

A hand appears in mine and instantly all my fear leaves. We seem to walk for some time, just enjoying one another's company. Suddenly, I notice that my hand has begun to slip in His, oil is flowing, the oil of myrrh is flowing out of a deep wound in His hand. His blood mingles with the blood from my scarred hands, the wounds seem as fresh as when I first cut them. The brokenness inside me begins to emerge at last and I crumple into His arms sobbing, throwing myself under the olive tree.

Time passes and I hear a clock ticking, each tick taking me back into my past, unravelling the carefully constructed walls that I had put up, walls to stop the pain, walls to stop the hurt.

I am back in the grand hallway, the grandfather clock ticking away encased in its gold richness, its wealth, looking down on those who pass under it. It stands in its arrogance and majesty enjoying the power it has over the minions.

I hear the whispers, I smell the candle wax and incense, I hear the children disciplined and shut up.

"Quiet please, quiet please, the service is about to begin!"

The performance begins, the voices trying to drown one another out, voices trained to perfection, voices speaking out the party line.

Hands reach out, out down the years, out down the centuries, gentle hands, loving arms cradling me again. The flicker of recognition as I begin to recognise that I have met this Person before.

CHAPTER 3
THE JIGSAW PUZZLE

I awaken to the sound of a trumpet call, it jars my consciousness and bullies me into listening. The sound is not pleasant and it disrupts my lovely dream. I don't want to listen to this call, I am happy the way I am. I am happy wallowing in my self-pity, if people want to reject me then I will reject them. The bitterness of the weed growing in my body, choking my organs, squeezing out every bit of life is left unchecked. I turn away from these unpleasant thoughts and reach out to listen to the church's latest teaching. Calm comes over me once more, I am back in my comfort zone, back on the wheel going round and round, going nowhere.

"Are you enjoying yourself?" The voice interrupts my reverie pulling me back into the present.

I am alarmed. "Of course, I am not enjoying myself, how can I, I feel so alone, so misunderstood, and I am sick and no one cares, no one cares at all."

"Hum, are you sure that is true?"

Suddenly, I am taken back, back to the quiet waters under the apple tree. He is there, smiling at me, His eyes lock into mine and I am enveloped in a comfort blanket of love, which takes my breath away. The weariness overtakes me and my tears begin to flow, they flow and flow as if the torrent inside me has at last been released and I don't know when I will ever be able to stop.

He just holds me, He says nothing. He doesn't try to play down my pain, He knows it has to come out, right out and be confronted, to be revisited before the healing can begin.

It starts again, this falling back into the past, the past blocking joy, blocking life.

I am back in our large lounge, the family is all gathered around, gathered together in grief. Our beloved mother is dying and it seems this time our prayers are not being answered.

I want to pray but as I speak up, my mother says no and looks horrified. Instead my younger brothers take up the prayer and I am silenced once more. Women are to be silent in all things spiritual it seems, even in our own home!

My heart hurts, the emotion welling up inside me is forced back down and my heart breaks open, the gaping wound leaking out continuously draining my body of energy.

As my mother lies on the slab in the mortuary, it's as if I have died with her. I bow in submission, my head covering jammed onto my head, my head aching with the onslaught of oppression.

I look down from above and I see myself lying in my Lover's lap. I see my head, I see my brain and it is clogged up with bits of a giant jigsaw puzzle that just don't seem to fit. My Lover is gently removing all this junk, these ill-fitting bits jutting out in sharp edges cutting into my head causing the pain.

"What are you doing,?" I ask in wonder as I feel the pain subside.

"I am removing all the wrong beliefs and the lies." He says matter-of-factly.

"Oh not again!"

"You, My bride , have eaten from the wrong tree, just as Adam and Eve did, most of My church is listening to the wrong voice. Most of My church doesn't know Me at all!"

I feel the warmth flood over my head, I smell the spiced oil as it drops down over me and seeps into every organ, every cell.

"Ooh, this is lovely!" I exclaim as He continues to love me.

"You are so very lovely, so precious, so beautiful to Me." He sings, of course I don't believe it!

The melody changes and climbs higher, and soaring notes come and join in, the different harmonies jumping and jiving within the song. A heavenly language that I cannot understand falls out from His lips and as He sings, the lies are thrown out and clarity comes at last. Of course He loves me, He loves me as a besotted bridegroom for His bride, He sees all my faults and loves me just the same.

I see the love oozing out of His eyes, I see that love wrap itself around me in a cloak, a cloak of purple, I am His inheritance, I am His queen.

I reach out and take the apple of refreshment He offers me, I reach out and eat the raisins, the dried grapes, the Holy Spirit infusing me with His strength. I sleep once again.

CHAPTER 4

THE HOLY DOVE AND THE BLACK CAT

"It's time to dance," He says pulling me to my feet. But must I get up? I am so comfortable here with my Lover, just the two of us exploring one another, learning more about love.

"The season has changed, My fair one, it is time to run in ministry with me up on the mountains of trouble. Come, I will guide you, I will show you the way."

He runs on ahead, I climb back into bed!

I awake with a start, the nightmare still fresh in my mind. The black cat had come and sat on my chest, I couldn't breathe, I was suffocating, I couldn't alert my husband next to me, he was fast asleep, I couldn't talk, no sound would come out of my mouth.

I was back in my childhood, the asthma and bronchitis had taken hold. I was struggling with every breath, fear moving its way stealthily through my body. The cat would send me into a fit of allergic reactions watching from the side of the bed, licking its lips with glee.

The black cloud of depression descended over me. It was only a dream, for goodness sake, what was the matter with me! There is no reason for me to feel this low. I blame it on a virus, but subconsciously I know better! Something is not right.

I sleep a lot, waking often in the middle of the night, desperate to find my Bridegroom again. I cannot find Him, wherever I look, He is not there. I attend church, I attend small groups, I read the bible, I listen to the sermons, but I feel dead inside.

Then one morning, He is there, sitting on the edge of my bed, bathed in light.

"I have banished the demon cat," He says, "the witchcraft attacking your mind. You must focus on Me and not the sickness and the darkness. Whatever you focus on you will empower. Remember, My bride, you have dove's eyes, eyes that focus only on what is in front of you. It is time to stop compromising, it is time to belong to Me fully. Come, I want to show you something in our secret garden."

My heart leaps in my chest, I am so relieved to be back with Him again. I take His hand and off we run, laughing towards the green meadow.

"My Father wants to meet you, Beloved, He wants to meet the one I call 'My very own'."

I am excited and in awe, I have never visited the throne room in heaven before. Suddenly, out from under the trees a figure comes dancing into the clearing where we are standing. He is dancing in a most ungainly manner, full of fun and laughter. Surely not, I feel rather offended, it seems most unholy, this can't be our Father, can it?

They grab my hands and begin to twirl me round and round. Their laughter is infectious and gradually my reservations melt away and I join in wholeheartedly.

I begin to laugh and laugh, I feel like I will never be able to stop, everything is so funny, absolutely hilarious. When I think of the seriousness of our church services, the quiet boredom suppressing all independent thought, I collapse in giggles again.

Oh dear, oh dear, we know nothing! We read our bibles, we talk about our Lord, but we don't know Him at all.

"Oh, and another thing, why do you ignore Me, when it is Me who is talking to you all the time?"

The voice, it is the voice, and yet Father and Jesus are still dancing. I look round perplexed, not knowing what to do. I feel a heat building up inside me, it bubbles up out of my mouth and materialises as a pinkish vapour, the outline of a figure that begins to join in the dance too.

"So there are three of you after all, You are not just the power?"

The guffaws that follow were enough to show up my ignorance a hundred fold. It is amazing to think that I have had a relationship with Holy Spirit for so long and yet I never knew it was Him.

An angel appears at my side and begins to show me how humility governs Holy Spirit. You don't hear much about

Holy Spirit because He always points to Jesus or to Father, but without Him their work would be impossible.

I feel exhausted, there was so much to take in. "Come, Beloved, it is time to sit under the apple tree again, deep healing is about to take place." I lie down gratefully next to the quiet waters and let the water lap gently at my feet.

CHAPTER 5

THE POWER OF THE BLOOD

I awake in the darkness, I hear the siren in the distance, it's noise pulling me out of the deep sleep, forcing me back into wakefulness. My mind hurts, it just never seems to switch off, I crave sleep's oblivion once more but the darkness seems to be fading. A light is pushing in through my closed eyelids rudely invading my space. There is a tinkling sound in the quietness that becomes clearer and louder. Suddenly, I am fully awake and I can smell a potent perfume, I am not entirely sure whether I like it or not. It seems to dull my senses and seduce me into passivity. There is a figure in my room, a figure full of light and yet there is a darkness at its source. I hear the seductive music again and I feel myself falling back into the sleep of the dead.

"No, help me, Jesus!"

In heaven, Jesus speaks.

"It is time to intervene, Abba, she is being sucked in again, I can't bear to watch this any longer, she has asked for Our help."

"Of course, My Son, go to her and show her what is happening."

I awake to the birdsong, a glorious symphony of beauty melting into the day. I lay there in my bed luxuriating in the quietness and stillness, unaccustomed as I am to waking so early. Memories from the night start to return to me and I feel afraid, very afraid. I get up and go downstairs to make myself a cup of tea. I reach for my phone and begin to text my friends asking for prayer. Weariness encloses me like a sheath and I feel unable to breathe properly. I know I am breathing, obviously, but I sense it is very shallow. I have always breathed like this, I have never known anything different and yet I just know this is a half-life, there is so much more.

I have to be with Jesus, I need to be with Him in our secret garden. I take my tea into the conservatory and sit with my journal waiting for Him to come. After a little while, He comes to me in my imagination, this time He comes riding on a white horse, He is carrying a large silver sword encrusted with rubies.

"Beloved, come with Me," and He invites me up onto the horse in front of Him. His strong arms enfold me and I feel as light as a feather, all the heaviness and weariness disappear instantly, I am alive like never before, all of a sudden my breath seems to be coming from a much deeper place. As we gallop off into the horizon, we seem to fall into another sphere entirely, we seem to be flying and we are not alone. I become aware of angels all around us, we seem to be in a translucent bubble. Outside this bubble there is another sphere or bubble and I start to see dark figures emerge with distorted gargoyle-like faces. Jesus grips me tightly and I am reassured that they can't touch me because I am with Him.

"Last night, you encountered that demonic sphere, My child. The supernatural world is not bound by time and space and there are times when we fall into other spheres. I allowed all this to happen, My precious girl, because of your desperation to know the truth, you grew up being told that the devil, witchcraft and the demonic were a deception, you needed to know that it is very real. However, once you know who you are, once you know how much I love you, once you know your inheritance as My bride, they cannot harm you ever again. I want to show you something."

Suddenly, I am taken back in time, back to the day of the crucifixion, back to the whipping.

I see the whip, the horrific instrument of torture containing many strands with a hard ball attached to each strand. I watch, appalled, as just one lash sent the balls blasting into my Lover's skin. I am zoomed into just one wound, from one ball, breaking the skin, the deep wound pouring out His life blood onto the ground. Suddenly, I am transported into this wound, I am swimming in His blood, I feel the hurt, I feel the pain, the pain of rejection by the people He came to save. I feel as if I am being washed out of this wound and I fall out onto the ground beneath the cross.

There is a heaviness, a blanket of darkness descending as I see the agony on the face of my Beloved. I scream out "No!" and a film appears in front of my eyes, a film of my life. I watch, horrified, as every act of sin, every act of compromise, every uncharitable thought, every time I stayed passive brought another slash of the whip blasting into my Beloved over and over again.

I crouch sobbing in the earth, aware of my filthy rags in a way I have never been aware of before. I look upwards and see His face, etched in an agony I cannot begin to understand. I see a cloak of sin cover my Jesus, sin that does not belong to Him. I see heaven close its door and the separation from His Father is complete.

The thunder roars, the lightning strikes as the life is extinguished from His body. The lightning illuminates His face one last time and I see the transformation, I see a love that I cannot begin to describe fall over that scarred, disfigured face. I see His chest rise up and those eternal words were expelled with His last breath.

"Forgive them, Abba, for they know not what they do!"

CHAPTER 6

THE DIVINE EXCHANGE

I am lying in His arms under the apple tree, the blossom sending out its delicate scent across the meadow. He is stroking my hair and singing softly and yet His eyes seem far away. This is not quite right I think, normally when I am with Him, I am the centre of His world, His focus is so fully on me and me alone.

"What is distracting you, my darling?" I ask tentatively.

He smiles at me and begins to speak. As He speaks, the love flowing out from Him is tangible, tears pool out of His eyes and rain unchecked down His cheeks.

"I came to earth in human form, I came to model a life for you to follow. I experienced everything that you all experience. The cross was the culmination of everything. What My church does not seem to understand is how wounded they are. They may not be physically wounded as I was, but emotionally and spiritually, they are in just as much mess as I was on that cross. Every unkind word is an arrow full of poison going straight into their hearts. They put up walls to protect themselves from hurt, but those walls keep Us out. We knock on their hearts constantly, asking to be let in, but most of them are so busy they do not even hear the knock anymore.

Holy Spirit is right in them, ready to be their Counsellor and take them through the stages of healing, but they look elsewhere, they turn to others or they push the pain down, they bury it believing that they are absolutely fine, and the tragedy of it all is, they believe their own lie! My church is full of the walking wounded, and yet they were meant to show others the way."

I don't understand. "But didn't the cross cover all this?"

"Of course, but people have to believe it. When you are wounded, you lash out at others and sin enters your hearts. My blood covered everything and as long as My people repent and believe they will receive the full divine exchange. I have done my part, but you must play your part. I have made you a promise and as long as you obey and love Us with all your hearts and love one another as yourselves, the full divine exchange will be unlocked for you."

"What is the full divine exchange?"

He begins to sing:

"It is time, time to receive from the throne
My beloved, My bride
Are you ready? Do you understand?
Come, come to Me
Let me return what the enemy stole
Come, come to Me

Let the victory unroll.
Righteousness for your sin
Healing for your wounds
Blessing for your curse
Abundance for your poverty
Acceptance for your rejection
Joined to God instead of separation
Life instead of death.
Take My hand
Come up higher
I invite you to know Me
Really know Me like never before.
Come, come with Me
Right into the Father's heart
Joined together by My blood."

CHAPTER 7
BACK TO EDEN

I am lying in bed, resentment pushing out of my pores filling the room with its ghastly stink. My husband lies next to me, fast asleep, satisfied, his gentle snoring rising to a crescendo of offense banging in my ears.

"What about me?" I think, "doesn't he care that I am not satisfied?" The pity party begins as I go over and over past hurts. Suddenly, I hear a song from the past running through my head.

'It's my party and I'll cry if I want to...'

Oh what now? I am really fed up and incredibly angry.

Suddenly, I am aware of Jesus sitting at the end of my bed again, He is laughing gently. I am incensed, what is so funny?

Then a strange thing happens, His laughter starts to affect me and in a matter of moments, I begin to crack a smile, this sends my Lover into guffaws of laughter, this laughter rolls over and rests on top of me and I am undone! I haven't laughed like this since my childhood, when my best friend and I were inseparable and drove people mad with our giggling.

After some time, when I am calm again, He begins to speak.

"Let Me show you what is really happening."

The film comes to life, my life as seen from heaven's perspective.

I see my wounds festering inside my body, emotional wounds giving rise to wrong thoughts and beliefs. I see a dark figure spewing forth lies into my head.

I see my husband as I have not seen him for a very long time, actually, if ever! I see him trying to please me every way he knows how. I see the words 'religious spirit' pop up over me and then I see how damaging that has been. I see that I have been programmed to believe that love making is a taboo and illicit affair, this has closed my body off to avenues of pleasure which are wide paths of colour encircling every part of me, I see that there is a sign at each avenue with the words 'No entry' typed in bold red.

I look over into Jesus' face, He is crying. "Keep looking!" He implores. I turn back to the film as if drawn by a massive magnet, I watch as our marriage is superimposed over two others. I just know they are Adam and Eve.

I watch them loving one another, I watch them loving and communing with God, there is a palpable joy brimming up out of their union. I understand at last that lovemaking between a husband and his wife is worship, the purest form of worship ever created, it is truly one flesh. As they become one flesh with one another, they become one flesh with their Creator, this is Holy Communion.

Shock waves flow through me, over and over, as Jesus tells me to keep on watching. I see the serpent tempting Eve, I see her bite the fruit, I see Adam, take the same fruit and bite into it.

"Eve was deceived, my darling, just as you were, Adam was not deceived, he knew what he was doing but chose to do it anyway. Both sinned, both turned away from Us. Before they were naked and unashamed, they had unbroken communion with Us and one another. That is why I was sent to earth to reverse the curse lying over the earth and to enable you to journey back to Eden with Me."

CHAPTER 8

COMMUNION

I am kneeling down at the communion rail about to take the bread and the wine. Just as I put the bread in my mouth I hear,

"SPIT IT OUT!"

I am so scared that it falls out of my mouth and onto the floor, I crumple into a heap on the cold stone floor. Rough hands usher me into the back room and I am told to be quiet and compose myself. I hear a waterfall of sobbing that cannot be stemmed, I am unaware until that moment that it is me making such a noise.

I seem to be transported to the courts of heaven where God is sitting on His throne as Judge. I see Jesus as my defence council at my side and then I see the accuser of men march forward.

"You cannot bless her, she is angry with her husband, she is bitter and is not reconciled with her brothers and sisters."

The angry words pierce my heart like a dart, tearing and ripping it apart. It stands there with its gaping wound and my heart knows that everything that has been thrown at me is true.

"I am so sorry, my Lord, I am so very sorry." I sob uncontrollably.

The accuser sits back with a self-satisfied smile on his face, his dark friends cheer from the balconies. One more on the way to hell, he seems to say, rubbing his hands together in glee.

Jesus stands, His presence pulsating light. He holds out His hands with the nail marks still marring His perfection. Blood is pouring out of His wounds, He reaches forward and takes my hands in His. His blood begins to poor into the wounds in my hands and above my head written in His burgundy blood are the words, 'PAID IN FULL'.

Jesus smiles down at me and says gently, "this is why so many in My church are sick and have died, they are taking communion in an unworthy way and bringing judgment down on themselves."

"Oh, Lord, forgive us for we truly don't know what we are doing!"

God the Judge looks down on me with kindly eyes and suddenly it is as if ties were removed from His hands and He turns into our loving Father, our Abba again. Suddenly, I see angels dispatched to bring me all the blessings that had been held in heaven waiting for me to understand. Justice has been done!

CHAPTER 9

PINK AT LAST

I am in the rose garden with Jesus our gardener. There has been so much pruning in the past season and although it is winter still, I can just begin to see buds starting to emerge. He wants to show me the yellow rose but of course I can't see it, not yet.

"You are My yellow rose, My sister, My bride. You pursue Me with intention, you have dove's eyes and nothing will side-track you from Me. There is no spot in you, you are opening up in complete abandonment, your aroma is My aroma, you fill up My senses. All pure are you and holy as I am holy."

I look at Him questioningly. He continues...

"And, now I have spoken it out, it will come true. All you have to do is believe and receive like a little child!"

"I believe and I receive." I say with enthusiasm and then I add "Oh, and help my unbelief."

He nods and says that is why we have come here to this part of the garden. It is time for some more deep healing.

I am falling again, like petals in the cold north wind. I seem to be in a dark tunnel and I am scared. I hear the voice speaking to me, telling me to trust Him, I feel His touch and I relax and let the events take their course.

I seem to be in a glass cot, my little feet and hands are inky blue with cold. My mother looks lovingly over me wanting to protect me from harm. She feels rather helpless and admits to herself the undeniable truth that she is a little disappointed not to have had a son, she feels that somehow she has been found wanting in not providing her husband with the son and heir he so desperately wanted.

My father, it seems has gone off to celebrate or commiserate with his football buddies and my mother is not really sure when he will return.

The nurse comes in and I hear her whisper to her colleague that it is a shame about the red hair! The bleeping continues in the special care baby unit and I am back in the tunnel again.

I am in our home and my father has just returned from work and he is tired. My mother ushers us all out of the way but I manage to escape and knock on daddy's study door. My knock is ignored or not heard and I sit on the stairs and the tears come.

Suddenly, Jesus appears by my side and asks me what I want to do. I say that I just want to play and with that a huge doll and pram appear out of thin air.

I am back under the apple tree in His arms, sobbing. The deep healing has begun, it is OK to want to play with dolls, it is OK not to want to play sport all the time, it is OK not to want to climb trees, play with cars and trains and most importantly it is OK to want to dance and sing and wear pink dresses.

A song begins:

"The feminine form is so divine
The soft contours of her body
Melt into mine
We are two but created as one
One flesh, one passion, one love.

Our differences are our strength
They complement one another perfectly
There is no join for we are one heart
There is no greater art.

The feminine form is so divine
The soft contours of her body
Melt into mine
We are two but created as one
One flesh, one passion, one love."

The song soars overhead, bringing peace and calm. The song, I see, is the journey back to Eden it is the journey back into worship, the journey back into love.

CHAPTER 10

ONE FLESH

We are lying in bed, my husband and I, lying in each other's arms. Today, I had him all to myself, no interruptions, no meetings, no sport! As I lie there in his arms, I feel so loved, so safe, so protected, I begin to feel that I really matter at last.

I am drifting off to sleep when I feel a click inside me, something has shifted deep down within me. I feel the heavenly arms enfold me and the song begins:

"You are My wife, My beautiful wife
Oh how I have longed to hold you
How I have longed to tell you just how much
I love and value you.
Don't be too busy for Me, My love
Stay still and let Me heal your broken heart
For your heart, My Beloved, is broken, broken
Right in two.
But be still in My presence and I will pour in My healing balm.
Those thorns stuck right into the heart of you
Those wounds which have penetrated so deep
Those wounds that have been hidden.

Now is the time that I have sovereignly appointed for
healing
Do not be too busy for Me, Beloved
Come and rest at My feet
Come and lay your head upon My chest

Listen to My beating heart, can you hear it?
Now listen to your own heart,
Put your hand over it
Do you feel it beating?
See, we are out of time.
Wait, be still, watch My face
Listen to My voice
Let Me minister deep inside you.

I want to be wherever you are
I don't want to ever leave your side
We are one flesh, you and I
See how our flesh is joining
No more pulling back
No more fear.
Let go, submit yourself to Me, Beloved
Let your blood mingle with mine
Let our bodily fluids join
We are one flesh, you and I
One flesh, joined forever by My blood
And by My Spirit."

Slowly I begin to trust
Slowly I begin to release
Slowly the walls come tumbling down
I am wide open, wide open
So very vulnerable

So very sore.
Gently, gently, I look into His eyes
Gently, gently, I allow His touch
Gently, gently, the caress begins
I focus on His eyes
His eyes loving me, penetrating
Deep down inside of me.
I reach out, reach out for my Lover
I am safe, I am loved, I am wanted.
I no longer feel used
I no longer feel disposable.
As I open up further
I begin to feel the release
The release building deep inside of me
Joy bubbles up within me
A swoosh of warmth invades every part of me
I feel alive, alive like never before
I reach out and touch His heart
I reach out and touch my heart
The wonder, the joy as the realisation of it all
Becomes clear
Our hearts beat in time once more
They move together as one
One flesh
One passion
One love.

I lie there in a haze of heavenly ecstasy. Something has changed, I have changed. I am no longer the girl running after every idol, I am no longer the girl putting men up on a pedestal, I am no longer the girl turning to mere people or things. I am loved, I am loved by the Creator of the world, I am loved and cherished by my Heavenly

Bridegroom. I matter, my identity is in Him. I know who I am at last, no more will I turn to others for affirmation. I don't need to people-please any longer, I am free, free to be me, free to be the woman that God always meant me to be!

A vision appears before my eyes, the NO ENTRY signs have been taken down. I see new pathways spring out from my mind and make their way all over my body.

"Your body was made for enjoyment, you are spirit, soul and body. I have been healing you in your soul, this is your mind, will and emotions. This has been the root cause of your lack of intimacy with Me and your husband. Now you know who you are, how loved you are, you will be transformed, you and all your relationships."

CHAPTER 11

THE WEDDING DRESS

I am walking outside the secret garden, when the wind begins to blow, it's gusts picking up the washing drying on the line, pulling it from under the pegs and it is strewn all over the muddy earth. I am dismayed, all the work I have done ruined in an instant even the careful hand washing! I am not amused, not amused at all. I go to gather up all the dirty clothes, when out of nowhere, I hear the voice.

"When will you stop? When will you stay still and listen? When will you find out what I want you to do?"

"But I have been working hard. I have so much to do, the church has been keeping me busy with its work and there is all the housework and shopping..." I trail off defensively.

"Let's talk about clothes!"

"What? What have clothes got to do with anything?"

Quite a lot it turns out. He begins to show me how clothes represent each person's calling, his or her destiny.

People are wearing clothes they were never meant to wear, they are ill fitting and just look awful.

He reminds me of the years that I taught Sunday school, I hated every minute of it!

"You were given the wrong dress to wear, My love. The church was fitting you into their mould, their way. They needed Sunday school teachers and they forced you into it. It did you no good at all, in fact it damaged your self-esteem further and those poor children were robbed of the teacher they should have had! There was someone who would have been a perfect fit, but because you filled in, they were robbed of the opportunity."

"But they were desperate!"

"Many people are so intimidated, they feel that they won't measure up, but if you give them time, if you encourage them, they will begin to shine."

"Well, what about all the years of cleaning toilets and making, tea, coffee and the dreaded baking?" I ask ungraciously.

"Everyone needs to serve others in humility before I can promote them."

Instantly, I see Jesus washing the disciples' feet and I feel well and truly convicted. Something begins to leak out of me, I am embarrassed!

"Don't worry, My love, it is just a bit more resentment leaving!"

He picks out a brown dress from the pile of dirty washing and holds it up in front of me.

"It is time for this to go," He says and throws it into the rubbish bin. I am cross, and I go to take it out again.

"I am very fond of this dress, my mother bought it for me."

He sighs. "I wanted to give you this instead," and hands me a large gift wrapped box.

I am rather taken aback and ever so carefully remove the pink ribbon and lift off the lid. Nestled inside a wad of coloured tissue paper is the most beautiful wedding dress I have ever seen. Well, I call it a wedding dress because my spirit recognises it as such and yet I have never come across such exquisite beauty in a garment before.

He begins to sing:

"It is time for Me to dress My bride
The bride called by My name
She is waiting
She is yearning
She is longing for more of Me.
I have been at work
Dressing her inside and out
But My bride, My beautiful bride
Has been waiting
Waiting in the wings.

Not much longer now, My love
Not much longer

As I shield you under My wing
As I enclose you and love you
And make you My own.
The veil is waiting
To protect you from prying eyes
This perfect, this pure
This most exquisite of brides.
The dress is being made
In folds of lace and brocade
Each stitch costs
Each pearl sewn just at the right point
The point of surrender
The point of fulfilment.

A big heart sweeps up its billowing hem
Joining it together
Clasped at the bosom
Faint hues of pink and accents of blue
The flavour of the seashore
The shell encased it its translucent beauty.

It is time for all the old clothes to be thrown away
It is time to bring in the new
The intoxicating perfume
The swirling oils
Seeping out...
Moving through the material
Filling every available space
Covering every curve.

This dress, My love, is moulded tight around you
You are even now being dressed by the greatest
Fashion designer who ever lived

It is time to dance with Me
It is time to remove the wedding veil
It is time to see what has been hidden
It is time to be amazed."

There I stand in front of the mirror
In all the finery that royalty can buy
And yet so very simple and elegant
So very understated.

I have been completely stripped bare
All I can see
All I can know
Is my Bridegroom on that tree
All I can see
All I can know
Is my Bridegroom hanging there
All I can see
All I can know
Is my Bridegroom
He is my passion
All I can see
All I can know
Is pure joy in the arms of my Beloved.

CHAPTER 12
THE GARDEN OF MY HEART

I am back under the apple tree, in our secret garden. I have begun to understand a kingdom truth. Everything is upside down in the Kingdom of God.
Everything is totally opposite to the world's way.
I realise that I have been getting in the Lord's way,
I have been preventing Him doing what only He can do!
I have been trying in my own strength to get healed up and to bring healing to others, but this was never God's intention.

He is our healer, He is the miracle worker. My job is to point people to Him, so they can find their own secret garden, their own intimacy, their own healing, their own calling.

I feel a tap on my shoulder and turn around to see a large figure radiating a golden glow. He smiles at me and hands me a golden pen and some parchment.

"It is time to write," He says and disappears. I look perplexed at the blank page but I can't write, I think.

"Yes, you can, trust Me and have a go!"

I begin to write.

Hear the roar of the waterfall in the distance
A gentle echo cascading over the rocks.
It can be quite comfortable sitting here at a distance
Hearing the roar, hearing the waterfall.
But it is time, My love, to come closer to the source of
that waterfall
The source of all things
The source of love.
It is time to stand on the edge
The pulse of the current reaches out and draws me in.
"Come, My love, do you trust Me?" sings the Lover of
my soul.
He reaches out His hand towards me
I close my eyes and put my hand in His.
In we step, into the raging waterfall.
The ice cold water swirls around me
As Jesus takes me deeper.
My foot slips, but Jesus is holding me.

I am lost underneath the water
Underneath the torrents and the noise
Lost in the warmth and stillness
Lost in the arms of my Lover.
Deep inside the waterfall
Here is all peaceful
Here all is still
Here I am engulfed in a love so divine
So beautiful, so holy that I cannot speak it out.
This love, it swirls through my body
Kissing each part, washing it clean.
Here in the centre of the waterfall

Is fullness of joy.
Joy bubbles up out of me, from deep within.

I see myself rising up in a bubble
Rising upwards out of the waterfall
I float through the air
I come to rest on top of an apple tree.
The bubble melts away and I am sitting on a branch
With Jesus. The birds are sitting all around us
Singing a beautiful melody.
I feel such joy and peace
Such love and pure happiness.

Jesus speaks.
"This is your garden, this is how I see you.

In our secret garden there is a cascading waterfall
Flowing straight from heaven to earth. You are in that
waterfall, bringing My Spirit to earth.

I rest in you and through you, I come to others.

When you are not in the waterfall

You will be found sitting in this apple tree with Me

Sometimes you will lie under my shade as I feed and
minister to you.

There are times when together we will tend your
garden, digging up, planting seeds, enjoying the flowers,
eating the fruit.

This garden is a beautiful wedding bower, an archway
filled with flowers whose scent stretches on and on,
intoxicating.

Here, I see angels helping to make beautiful bridal
gowns, all are different. When one is finished, they hand
it to me." I look at Jesus and He says, "Come with Me,
it is time to dress a new bride," and together we go to
minister to one of his precious brides.

"This is your garden, this is your ministry. You are to help prepare the bride, you bring her to her own garden, her own apple tree, her own waterfall. To begin with, it will be a small brook, but it will grow into a river, a lake or a waterfall.

This is your ministry, a ministry of rest and restoration. Welcome to the garden of My heart."

Understanding overwhelms me as I put my pen down and the tears come again. I do fit into this body after all, I do have a part to play. I also realise with a start, that if everyone was made like me, nothing much would get done, but as part of the Body of Christ as a whole, I have a role and it is a vital role, it is intimacy. A picture of my breasts and genitals are suddenly thrust into my consciousness, and I begin to laugh.

"Oh dear, oh dear, I am not sure how the church is going to like this, it seems so irreverent and yet I know it is the most holy thing, it is Holy Communion."

CHAPTER 13
THE ONE NEW MAN

I seem to be in a church service, sitting quietly in one of the pews at the back of the church. I am concentrating on the message being taught, but I am finding it difficult to comprehend. The meaning of the Greek and Hebrew words are pointed out to me in great detail and the academic prowess of the speaker is highlighted to all who are listening.

The trouble is I am not entirely sure how many are still listening, many of us have drifted off, thinking about more mundane things such as food and our Sunday roast.

"Are you enjoying your food?" I hear out of nowhere. I feel guilty and caught out, He appears at my side.

"No, I mean are you enjoying your spiritual food?"

"Well, I would if I could understand it," I say sadly.

"Hum, yes I understand that would be a bit of a blockage. I wonder if Paul's teaching on speaking in tongues has been truly understood!"

"The intellect and excessive reasoning seems to have taken over from simple faith," He continues.

"Would you like Me to show you how it was in the beginning?"

I start to answer, but before I can get anything out of my mouth, I am transported back in time.

We are sitting on the floor in someone's home, people are crowded into the small room, sitting, standing, wherever there is space. There is a buzz of excitement running through the congregation as they wait for one another.

A man begins to sing as tears run down his beard, the emotion is thick and tangible. He sings of his love for his Saviour, his Saviour who had healed his crippled daughter. His daughter gets up and begins to dance. The joy bubbling out of her is contagious and suddenly everyone starts to follow her as she dances out into the street. This joy cannot be contained, this euphoria is like a bottle of pop just about to explode. Out they all go singing and dancing spreading the good news of the Kingdom of God.

They go out into the market place, they go out into the fields, in fact this church infiltrates every part of society. I watch as they embrace the poor and the sick, I watch as their love moves them out towards the outcasts, towards the misfits, the prostitutes, the tax collectors.

I see that this church is not a building at all, it is the people. I see that theirs is not a religion but a relationship, I see that there is no hierarchy but an equality which recognises each member as important. This church honours and respects each part of the body and encourages one another in their work.

"Unless you become like a little child, you will not enter My Father's house. I have modelled everything for you to follow, I have sent you the Holy Spirit to guide and teach you. I only did what I saw My Father do, you, My child, must do the same.

So many of My church do not have a relationship with Me, they idolise the Bible or the Torah, but it is only the road map to the Author."

"The Torah?" I ask bemused.

"It is time to come into a new place in our secret garden, it is time to visit the olive grove." He says.

The wind wraps around my body, whirling and twirling like a tornado. I feel squeezed in every direction as the momentum carries me forwards, the motion sickness of my past summersaults me into oblivion.

I am in the back of our family car, squeezed between two of my brothers, our haphazard journey down the narrow country lane ends abruptly as we come crashing through a hedge and land upside down in front of a huge tree. I get up rather shakily, still feeling decidedly queasy.

"I am so confused," I admit when I see Him smiling down at me from the branch of the very old tree.

"Have an olive!" He says as He throws a handful of this precious fruit over to me. I catch one and put it into my mouth.

"It's funny but I never used to like olives until recently," I mumble, my mouth dripping oil down my chin.

I am suddenly aware that my mouth is being continuously filled with oil and I have to keep swallowing.

Holy Spirit watches with amusement and tells me to watch carefully.

The huge olive tree seems to come alive in front of me. I see its huge trunk and suddenly I can see right through it. I see two chambers of light rising up from the base, I notice that one goes right down into the roots while the other one joins in about halfway up the trunk. They merge together for a short time then they seem to separate again.

They continue to lie side by side, not touching, both seemingly emerged in their own little world. I look closer and as the branches branch out I see how they have followed two very different and distinct paths. A television appears in the bottom of the tree trunk and miraculously it springs to life.

I see two families, one Jewish and one Christian and both are worshipping in their own ways. I see the Christian family turn on the Jewish family with hate and persecution. I see the Jewish family covered in scars, so scarred are they that they remind me of Jesus on the cross.

I see how the Jewish family have been so wounded and rejected that they have put up walls around themselves, determined to keep everyone out who might hurt them again.

I look at Holy Spirit needing more revelation.

"Christianity has its roots in Judaism, Jesus came to earth as a Jew, He lived and died as a Jew. He is both the Jewish Messiah and the Christian Messiah. He celebrated all the Jewish festivals, as they are not just Jewish festivals, they are God's festivals. They are appointed times, times when God wants to break into our world with the miraculous.

The Christian Church has taken on pagan festivals such as Christmas and Easter. However, we are so thrilled when you worship Us, it does not matter to Us, but we just don't want you to miss out on all the blessings associated with those appointed times.

"Do you know who the Bride of Christ really is?" He asks me.

"Well, it is the church and every individual believer," I answer.

"Yes, but first of all, before the church was born, it was Israel, Israel is My firstborn."

As the oil flows through my mind, the shutters are removed from my eyes and I see the truth for the very first time.

"Jesus can only return when His bride has prepared herself and is reconciled to her brothers and sisters. Her brothers and sisters are not only the Jewish people but every Christian denomination too.
    There is only one church, Jew and Gentile joined together in unity. Jesus gave His life on the cross to bring

all the divisions down. He gave His life to birth a new church, a One New Man Church where we can honour and respect one another and most importantly, where we can learn from one another.

You all only know in part, and if you would only come together with each part operating in its God given calling, you would have a much fuller picture than the fragments that you have at the moment. And remember, unity doesn't mean uniformity!"

CHAPTER 14
THE AIR BALLOON

Oh no, I am falling again, falling back into the past, I feel as if I am travelling down inside the trunk of a large tree. It is dark and the helter skelter ride is both scary and dangerous. Weeds jut out and entangle themselves in my hair, the pain is excruciating as the roots are tugged out in clumps as I continue helplessly on my journey to the bottom.

I arrive at my destination bleeding, balding and badly messed up.

I seem to be in a holiday park and it is Halloween weekend. Witches and wizards, pumpkins and popcorn scream out their wares, seducing the innocent to taste the sickly sweetness of their counterfeit reality.

I cannot sleep even though the cabin is perfectly comfortable. I lie awake for ages and then I reluctantly get up knowing that I can't pretend anymore. I have been hit with a metaphorical plank in my eye too many times to count lately. The judging has to stop, it is time to eat humble pie and apologise.

A funny thing happens when you apologise, a clump of hair starts to grow back and one of the chains is released inside you, leaving you in a rather lopsided position that moves you to do it again until you are level and the motion sickness stops.

Freedom takes time, I see, it is a journey into love, one act of loving kindness after another.

I see a big red air balloon and the basket is tied to the floor securely. There are two large weights in the basket keeping it down. I see that there are words written over these weights in a dull greyish black print.

One says RELIGION and the other says WITCHCRAFT.

"Come," says Papa God, "come sit on My lap and let me show you something." He picks up the weight with RELIGION written on it and turns it over. Written clearly on the back is WITCHCRAFT. Then He picks up the other weight with WITCHCRAFT written on it and turns it over and there it is lit up in bright psychedelic light RELIGION.

"It is time to throw both these weights out of your basket, My daughter. You were born to fly, you were born to be free, you were born to worship Me in spirit and truth."

A prayer rises up out of my belly and seems to fasten itself to the red balloon, as I speak it out, the balloon begins to rise gently in the sky.

"Loose the Tongue of Heaven over your people, Lord loose the language of worship and awe upon us,
I beseech you, Lord.
For we are a piteous people

We flounder and perish due to lack of knowledge
Have mercy upon us, my God.
Fill our mouths with Your words
Infuse our bodies with worship from the throne room
Let us become living sacrifices laid down for You.

May You become the reason we get up in the morning
May You be the sole purpose of our existence
May each breath we take be filled with You.
May You be our comfort, our shelter
Our anchor in times of trouble and turmoil.
As this precious language of heaven is released over and
in us
May our joy bubble up and join in the Song of all Songs.
May the melody and the harmonies join together
Rising over the roof tops in an unending crescendo
Drowning out the darkness as worship transcends space
and time.
Bringing us to our knees before your throne
Where every tribe and tongue will join together
In beauty and unity,
Singing of the One whom we all love
The One who laid His life down for us
The greatest sacrifice of all time
Love never ending...
Love never ending...
Going on and on forever into eternity."

CHAPTER 15
MY DELIGHT IS IN YOU

We are talking, my Lover and I, as we sit together in our rose garden. A lot of work has taken place here over the last three years, a huge amount of weeding and pruning but also new soil has been laid. The old soil just didn't seem to produce much at all, everything seemed diseased and stunted. Now I am amazed at the result. I see lots of different varieties of rose, each with its own distinct flavour, its scent permeating the atmosphere around it beautifully. What is wonderful about this garden is how all these different varieties blend in so beautifully together, there is no dominant aroma or colour to steal the show. Instead they are like a finely tuned orchestra, all playing their part to perfection.

"Watch!" He says as I see a little yellow rose lifted up. It seems to grow up out of nowhere. It opens its petals wide and begins to sing the most exquisite song imaginable. I am stunned.

"Keep watching!"

The beautiful yellow rose seems to bow over and then shrinks back into the undergrowth and the palest, most delicate of pink roses takes its place. Arms seem to grow out of its flower and a violin is produced and it begins to play. What is so extraordinary, however, is that the flower is holding the violin and yet the bow seems to have a life of its own, running across the strings and bringing new depths of sound that I have never heard before.

A rhythm is building from the earth and out pops an orange rose full of bold beauty. I am surprised at its confidence but when it starts its drumming, I am undone. What is happening to me? I crumple over sobbing and there is a huge wrench, a battle of extraordinary proportions is going on inside me. I see a robin hand Jesus a key. He looks at me kindly and says "It is time, My love, it is time to set you truly free, are you ready?"

I nod, words are impossible as I understand *that I have been on the throne* of my heart and not MY LORD. I am mortified as I see the truth at last.

Ever so gently I see His hands reach inside my heart, I feel the key inserted and the lock turned.

All hell is broken loose as the screaming begins. I am falling again, falling back into my twisted past, the counterfeit reality that had held me prisoner on her web of deceit.

We are excited as we wait to be invited up onto the stage, our hearts puffing up with our importance. Oh what a show we will give them, showing off our holiness, our prophetic words and healing gifts. The miracles and healings will take place and our fame will grow.

We have such a busy schedule for there is so much to be done, so many people to save, so many countries to visit!

The sobbing gets louder and louder and eventually peters out into exhaustion. I am lying once again in my Lover's lap under the apple tree. He is hugging me fiercely and singing softly into my ear.

"My delight is in you, My bride
My joy is to look into your eyes
And yes, to see the adoration staring back at Me.
You are My joy, My love, My perfect one.
Oh how beautiful you are
How I love to hear you sing to Me
Our own special love song
Written from heaven just for you and Me.
Come, let us sit together under the shade
Of the apple tree
Let My blanket cover you
Let Me feed you apples and raisins
As our love takes over.

My delight is in you, My bride
My joy is to see the choices you make
You always try to choose Me first
You ravish My heart, My sister, My bride.
I am melting under your gaze
As you turn your eyes towards Me again
I am lost, lost in YOU
Lost in the beauty and wonder of YOU.
The one I loved back to life
The one who fills up My senses
The one I call My own.
Two hearts beating as one
Joined forever, bound together
In the Father's love

Redeemed forever through My blood
Welded tight by the Holy Dove
Spirit to spirit
Soaring through the skies
Rising upwards, forever straining
Straining for more.
My delight is in you, My bride
Never forget My delight is in YOU."

I am overwhelmed by His love and mercy and can only
say, "Why?"

"You are the reason I chose to come to earth, there is a
battle going on which is so much bigger than you know.
A battle between good and evil, between God and the
devil.

My bride is under attack from the devil, for he knows
his time is short. His schemes remain exactly the same as
they ever were. He brings people down through three
main things:
Power and Pride
Greed and Wealth
Sex and Lust

When My bride turns away from sin, nothing can
harm her for she is protected by My blood. No demon,
principality or power can come near the blood, the devil
has no power at all. But if she compromises and listens
to the lies then her master becomes the prince of darkness
and his yoke is so very heavy. No one can stand up
under it.

For those who enter their own secret garden and move
through into the Holy Place and then into the Holy of

Holies, nothing can touch them, for I will be living in them in manifest form. Nothing will be impossible for them, they will move out in power, and together we will heal the sick, cast out demons, feed the hungry and raise the dead.

This is the key to the end time church, complete unity with God and fellow believers and a love for My firstborn, My Israel. The Jews are no better than you, but it is the divine pattern, just as the husband is first and then the wife and yet they are equal. It all boils down to obedience, obedience even when not fully understanding, this will bring the most amazing blessings to My church. But while she is still wounded, the holiness cannot come, healing must come first, then I will refine and sanctify her and she will be holy as I am holy, washed by the Living Word.

I am the Word made flesh, I came because man and woman could not win against the supernatural forces of darkness, however, when you eat of Me, when you allow Me to wash you with My words, those I speak to you directly and those written in the bible, then you begin to transform. All My supernatural qualities will be passed on to you, for everything I have is yours. You are marrying into royalty, you will have favour with God and man.

So submit, My love, do not fight against Me any longer, come and lie down in green pastures by the quiet waters and let Me heal your soul. Let Me renew your mind and give you My mind, let Me mend your broken heart and pour in My healing balm to restore every organ and cell.

I will heal you from the inside out, I will not just treat the symptom, but I will go to the root of the problem. Only when you are broken can I really use you, only when you know My perfect love will you be fearless and be able to do what I call on you to do, only when you know how much you are loved will you be able to love Me as I should be loved and only then will you be able to love others as yourself."

CHAPTER 16
PINK BALLET SLIPPERS

We are walking through the meadow quietly holding hands. We have not spoken for some time and I know Jesus is allowing me time to digest all I have heard. We walk through the little white gate and I can hear the roar of the waterfall in the distance. We had been walking for some hours and I suddenly realise that I am not remotely tired, how strange, normally I would be exhausted walking only a fraction of that distance.

I look at Him and He smiles, knowing my thoughts.
   "You are walking alongside me now, you are just doing what I show you, My yoke is light and not heavy at all!"

I look at Him and in shock and surprise blurt out, "So you mean to tell me that it has taken me most of my life to learn to do NOTHING, NOTHING AT ALL!"

He starts to laugh as if He will never stop but eventually He composes Himself and answers.

"Well, yes and no. It is all about resting and waiting and being ready to step out only when you see Me stepping out. It is about obedience and doing what I ask you to do, when I ask you, and how I want you to carry it out.

You have made the same mistake as many of My precious ones, and that is to do the right thing but at totally the wrong time. This can have catastrophic results as I have not yet carried out the work in the hearts of those you are ministering to and so they are unable to receive your word.

It is quite simple really, Beloved, you just have to become child-like again and follow your Daddy and do what He says. He knows what is best for you, He sees the full picture, you only see in part. It is all about trusting in Us when there is nothing and no one else to help you, it is total surrender."

The music begins to play and its notes pick up my hair and playfully begin to arrange it in a cascade of curls falling down my back. The quavers come back and pin in the jewelled clips to hold my hair in place. As we continue walking I become aware of my clothes for the first time in what seems ages. I am surrounded in what I can only describe as a wedding gown and yet it seems to be in every colour of the rainbow, its colours flowing gently into their neighbour's effortlessly. An intoxicating perfume is released from each hue, sending my senses into a quiver of delight. I feel like dancing, I pick up my dress and then I stop in my tracks in horror as I see my feet. My feet are encased in what I can only describe as broken black ballet shoes, the elastic across the bridge of my foot digging dangerously into my skin. My Bridegroom picks up a gift box and hands it to me.

I look at Him expectantly, I seem paralysed, I can't seem to reach out and take this free gift offered to me.

I seem to be in a trance and I am watching myself from above.

Jesus seems to become three in an instant and they form a circle around me protecting me under their wings. I am about to meet THE FAMILY.

I am sitting on DADDY'S lap, we are sitting in front of a mirror. He is telling me how beautiful I am and pointing out all the gifts and talents that He has planted in me. He shows me how he created me in my mother's womb with just the right DNA from each of my earthly parents and a huge download of divine DNA from my Heavenly Parents.

"You were born into a beautiful loving family on earth, you were very privileged to have such a family. You learnt about love and sharing in a way many others were never to experience. Religion tried to destroy you and tear your family apart but We intervened. For you see, My child, you were born for such a time as this, if you had not been through all this turmoil, you would not have been able to fulfil the destiny that We had marked out for you from before the creation of the world."

Suddenly, I am back in Devon with 26 of my family. I see us taking the bread and wine together for the very first time. The love is palpable, the tears close to the surface, my joy complete. The Holy Dove swoops over us and begins Her song which is also mine:

My heart is so full
I don't know where to begin
To say thank you and sing 'Praise the Lord'
Does not begin to cover it.

The aching in my heart has stopped
The longing turned to reality
My heart is so full
I don't know where to begin.

My mourning has turned to dancing
My despair changed to joy
The joy of being part of this family once more
The joy of reconciliation
The joy of belonging.
I could not function fully apart from you
Apart from you, I died inside
Cut off, isolated, estranged.

We are family, a royal family
United together through the blood of Jesus
United together in hope
United together in love.

My heart is so full, full to overflowing
Resurrection life flows through my veins
Jesus came to give us life and
Life in abundance.
The victory is His
The red carpet belongs to Him
We kneel in adoration
All glory to our King.

The Holy Dove lands softly on my head, turning into a feminine form holding a signpost. As She rests on me, I begin to change, my heart begins to melt and my eyes begin to see. She begins to point the way, teaching and nurturing me as a mother would teach her precious child.

"Come away with Me, it's time to meet your Bridegroom, the wedding supper has been prepared."

The Song begins to play, but this time it is accompanied by the whole orchestra, its symphony is moving to a close, a crescendo is coming, the finale is approaching The bride is waiting for her Bridegroom.

A film set comes to life, it is multimedia, cinematic and 3D. I am drawn in, helpless, just watching as I see our lives from heaven's perspective.

Broken vases smashed upon the pavements of life
Barbed wire on top of walls being built higher and higher.
Just one more job to be done and then the day is Yours
They promise
But one job follows another
A game to play, a show to watch
A book to read.
Papers piled up, higher and higher.
I wait patiently for My love to notice Me
I wait, and woo her gently from a distance.
The north winds begin to blow and My love
Begins to slow down, her back hunched up
Against the cold.
Surely she will turn to Me now?
Alas, no, she walks in the opposite direction

Lavishing her love on idols
Prostrating herself on the alters of religion and power.
I see the bleeding hearts as they pump their blood around
the body.
There is no strength, not enough to pump around to the
outer parts
They conserve their energy by pumping blood just into
their inner circles
Necrosing flesh as extremities begin to die.
Those outcasts on the edge
Isolated and alone
Left to fend for themselves
Left alone to die.

They come, these outcasts
These forgotten ones
They come crawling on their hands and knees
Crawling, begging, desperate for food
Crawling, begging, desperate for love.

At last! I sigh, at last they are looking for Me!
I am their last resort and yet I am their salvation.
I am their God, their strong tower in times of trouble.
I open wide the doors and welcome them in.
Come, My friends, come
Come and eat the finest of fare
Come, My friends, come and eat
From the King's richest table.
Come, My friends, come and drink
Drink deeply of the finest wines
Come in, come in, all are welcome.

Luxurious baths await us
Finest linen garments of all colours and hues
Silks and wools and all manner of costumes
Mantles made especially for each one
Tailor-made to fit to perfection.
Beautiful sandals are laid out for our feet
And tables of jewels for us to try on
Servants to help dress our hair
And bring us our clothes.

The perfume hits us as we wander through the rooms
Gentle aromas of flowers, scents tickling our noses
As we pass
Heady spices and sweet fruits intoxicating our senses.
We pass through to the banquet hall
A wedding is in progress
Much joy and laughter
I begin to feed hungrily
And drink as if I have never drunk before.
I expect to be turned out soon
It must have been a mistake, so I am going to make the
most of it.
I eat and drink my fill and then I lie down on the beautiful
comfortable cushions to sleep.

Time passes, I hear singing in the distance
A lullaby, a love song
A memory stirs, a memory from the past
A caress touches my face
I flinch
But the hand continues to caress me gently
I open my eyes and I am lost
Lost in the most beautiful soft eyes that I have

Ever seen.
Pools of love, pools of compassion
Melting the walls around my heart
"Come, My bride, I have been waiting."
He is talking to me, there is no one else here,
I just looked!
He gives me a beautiful coat of many colours
And as I put it on
I suddenly know who I am
Who I was always meant to be
The Lord's favourite, the Beloved,
The Bride of Christ, anointed!
This wedding feast, it is for ME!
I am the bride
Jesus is the Bridegroom
The Lover of my soul.

I stand still, the gift box still in front of me. Now, however, I know who I am, I am worthy, I am loved. This is not a hoax, someone mocking me from my past, this is love's free gift.

I open the box and inside I see them... The sob begins from deep down within me, the dream belonging to the little girl who used to be me comes flooding back.

My dream of being a ballerina, dancing effortlessly on point, the dream of dancing on and on, round and round, a dance of worship, a dance of love for an audience of One.

Strong arms guide me to the bench and He bends down and removes my old way of life, throwing the old broken shoes into the bin. He slides on the soft pink ballet slippers, and moulds them gently to my feet.

He ties the ribbons and asks me to stand up on point.

Well this could be interesting, I think, I absolutely expect to fall over and find it painful. I have seen how much practice it takes for ballerinas to train to stand on point and even longer to dance gracefully.

But I am determined to try, I am in love and I will do anything I can to please Him.

He helps me up and then once He sees that I have my balance, He lets go. I begin to twirl and the leaves from the trees are carried with the wind and wrap themselves around me and join in the merry dance. I am exhilarated as I find that it is easy, I was born for this, to dance with abandon for my Lover.

I dance round faster and faster holding onto my Lover, we seem to melt into one. The rushing roars through my ears, the water is all around us, gushing and rushing, bubbling and gurgling. We seem to be in the middle of the waterfall falling from heaven to earth.

The rainbow waterfall full of His promises, the blessings from heaven washing out onto the land, healing and restoring, reconciling and rewarding, flowing out of heaven over ALL who will say YES.

The drums beat under the earth, the rumbling has begun
The birth pains of creation's song
The song to usher in the King of Creation

The notes begin to push their way upwards
Upwards through the earth

The notes cut through the roots, weeds, stumps
And trees

The notes soar upwards called by their Creator
The Song of all Songs has released its music
Its notes of love calling forth to those beneath.

The canopy of heaven sparks its firework display
The symphony building, bubbling up with excitement
The excitement of the beloved as she goes to meet her
Lover.
She leaps like a firework all lit up with heaven's splendour.
As she pushes up and out of the earth
Her mouth opens wide and her voice is released.
The sweetest, loveliest voice
A voice full of love
A voice full of compassion
Calling to the others
Calling them to taste of the sweetest of fare
Calling them to love divine instead of despair
Beauty for ashes, beauty for ashes
Yes, that's the deal.

It is time to burn, burn up with our Lover
It is time for love's greatest rescue
Love's greatest miracle
As we rise up, renewed from the earth
Our ashes scattered on the breeze
A crown of beauty is laid ever so gently
Upon our heads

A bridal garland of intoxicating perfume
Flowers of every colour and hue

Every tribe and tongue
The garland of the bride
The song of the bride
As she makes herself ready
To meet her Bridegroom.

CHAPTER 17

SAFE HAVEN

I am sitting in bed enjoying my early morning cup of tea. I love this part of the day, this time with my Lover before the interruptions of the day invade this safe haven of peace and tranquillity. In this place, this secret place of deep communion with Him, I receive what is in His heart for me that day.

I sit with my journal in front of me, recording the dream I had been given overnight. I don't always understand but in the process of trying I often get an insightful bible study tailor-made for me that day!

For years I was led astray by turning to dream interpretations from others, looking up this and that and walking down the devil's footpaths of confusion.

There is nothing wrong with getting help, but the source of that help needs wisdom. I could never remember my dreams and in fact mistakenly thought that I didn't dream. But, of course, we all dream, and when the alarm clock rudely awakens us, everything falls away running down the drain of our consciousness, never to return. I now understand that if we are able to come to, slowly, we can catch those precious fragments before they drain away. I always keep a pen and notepad by my bed now and jot things down as they come to me.

Psychiatrists have known for years the importance of dreams in our healing but when we at last ask the giver of the dream for the interpretation, it all becomes so much easier and less time consuming. I have learned to meditate on them as I go about my day and often a revelation will open up to me like a flower opening up in the sunlight.

I love that I dream so often now, I love how it helps me understand things that I wouldn't know otherwise, I love how dreams from the past which I could make no sense of at all, knock on my consciousness, pushing me to revisit them and understanding comes at last.

There is a creaking sound, a whiff of stale air as the trap door of my past opens once more. Oh no, not again, I think, but it is too late the putrid air has wrapped itself around me and jettisoned me down into the pit of darkness and desperation once more.

I watch sadly as I am given false dreams from the enemy, dreams to cause conflict and strife and drive me further into the isolation of the rejected. I watch as pride puffs me up like an obese balloon spiralling me into the air, sending me further and further out into realms of a false reality, a deadly delusion of the religious fanatic!

The dreams themselves have become an idol, my foot is well and truly caught. The spider's web of lies bounces me about like a helpless fly, the spider is about to move in for the kill.

I am so very scared crouching on the damp ground in the bottom of this deep pit, the pit of my own making.

The rats running over my toes send me into a spasm of fear that paralyses me and my breathing becomes erratic, the pain in my chest is excruciating and begins to radiate down my arms. The boulder inside my heart begins to break as the lightning burst erupts into my consciousness. The storm has begun, the storm sent to bring me back to my senses, the storm sent to save me from this madness, the storm of compassion sending me out of the rough seas of religious mania and back into the harbour of love, the safe haven of truth.

I sit rather shell-shocked on the corner of my world.
I sit beneath the apple tree bathed in a blanket of His love, my Saviour, my Deliverer, my Beautiful Lord.
I sit rather shell-shocked in the aftermath of the battle, the grand old battle to set the people free.
I remember another tree,
I remember another woman
Another lured by the serpent, just like me.
We tasted of that forbidden fruit, she and me
I can still taste the poison in my mouth
It tasted so sweet at first, but grew into a bitter weight
As it hit my stomach
Dragging me further and further down into the pit.

The seduction had begun, drawing me deeper and deeper onto the intricacies of her web.
Spinning lie after lie, counterfeit after counterfeit
Destroying, stealing, killing everything that was good.
Confusion was the order of the day.
A false reality stealing every independent thought

A fogginess in my brain, where all I could think about
was ME, poor old me.
I was the centre of this world

I saw only from one perspective, MINE.
Blindness crept upon me gradually,
The deafness followed straight behind.
The chains wrapped themselves around my ankles
The stone in my heart began to grow.
I was lost in the pit, lost in the madness
Lost in the seduction of an evil
An evil I had not believed.

I looked across at those eyes I love
Those eyes that melt with love
Every time I look into His face.
My rescuer, my Jesus,
My Lover, my all.

He could not leave me there
His love was too strong to bear
His love was such that He had already given
His life for me
Long, long ago on another, different tree.
His blood had paid the price
He was just waiting, waiting and
Waiting some more.

What was He waiting for, Beloved?
Before He reached down to lift me out of the pit
The pit of my own making!
He sent warnings, dreams, people, scripture
But I wallowed there, stubborn and sticky
In my own mess and mire.

Time passed, I am not even sure how it happened
But slowly, ever so slowly
The veil was stripped away
Little by little, I began to see
Clarity came at last
Along with the inevitable heartbreak.

The heavens were rent, the thunder crashed
The lightning came like a double edged sword
Targeting my heart in light and mercy.
My knight in shining armour had come at last
To rescue me from my enemies,
My foes, who were too strong for me.

What was He waiting for, Beloved?
Why did He tarry so long?
He was waiting, waiting ever so patiently for me.
A broken and a contrite heart is the key
As soon as your heart breaks
As soon as you see your filthy rags
As soon as you cry out in repentance
And ask for mercy
He comes, He comes immediately
He comes with love, a love that breaks your heart
Over and over again.

He scoops you up on His white horse and carries you
To His secret garden, the garden of love
Where, for a season, you will sit and taste of the
sweetest fruit
The fruit of goodness
The fruit of kindness
The fruit of healing

The fruit of refreshing.
Do not hurry love during this set-apart time
For during this time
You will get to know your Saviour as never before.
It is time to fall in love.

CHAPTER 18
TIME TO EAT PLUMS

"It is time to eat some plums!" I hear as I turn into our driveway. We have been away with some friends on holiday, a Croatian cruise into the turquoise transparency of a crystal clear sea. It is lovely going away but there is always something special about returning home, home to the quietness and stillness, home to uninterrupted time with Him.

I have changed, the girl who forever craved company has long gone, the company I crave now has spoiled me for every other. Don't get me wrong, I love being with others, I love spending time with friends and family, I love meeting strangers who delight me with their differences. But the centre of my world has to be Him, always Him, the adventures I have, the excitement of learning and experiencing the supernatural with my Jesus makes our earthly world decidedly dull.

I no longer need the excitement of alcohol, shopping, novels or films to entice me into a fantasy world, I am part of a supernatural world, I was created to be supernatural, I was created to create.

I rush around, unpacking and getting us something to eat. For once, it is just my husband and I at home, the children are all away, we have the place to ourselves. It seems such a novelty to have space and time after the slightly cramped cabin on the boat, so nice to breathe our own air without the gentle influence and sound of others dancing around our heads.

I am excited about eating plums although I am not really sure what that means, but I sense Holy Spirit has something to do with it! At last I sit down quietly waiting for Him to show me what is to happen next. I wait, and wait and then I wonder why nothing is coming. Suddenly it dawns on me that I haven't asked Him yet? Of course, why didn't I think of that sooner. It is a relationship after all, not a religion.

He laughs gently in my ear and whispers my husband's name.

"Well, what does that mean?" I ask impatiently. Suddenly I am reminded of a lovely man from my past who came with an important message for me.

"DO NOT FORGET YOUR EARTHLY BRIDEGROOM AS YOU GO AFTER YOUR HEAVENLY BRIDEGROOM."

Suddenly, the cloudy waters become clear and I realise how I have pushed my beautiful husband out of the way. He suggested that we go to bed, but in my busyness and super spiritual way I packed him off to his study. Afternoons have always been the best time for love making as far as I am concerned, a haven of time where nothing has to be rushed, time for some foreplay and tender words. I am taken back to the first years of our life together, that precious time before religion took its hold.

Time before the children came along, time when we had quality time with one another, time to explore one another's bodies. I was always a bit repressed, I see, even then, but God has been opening both our eyes.

During our holiday, my husband lost me for a while, he was jolted to see how much he loves me. We have both taken each other for granted, but God is doing a deep work in us.

Suddenly, I see the parallels, the parallels between the heavenly marriage and our own. I see how Jesus has gently wooed me, I see how my husband has been doing the same. I see how Jesus will not come in until I am ready and invite him in, I see how my husband is beginning to do the same. I see how I am opening up in a love that knows no limit, an abandoned love which I have yet to taste. When perfect love comes, there is no fear, no resentment, no hasty fumbling before Match of the Day begins or before going off to work.

Love takes time, it takes commitment, it is patient and kind, it never puffs itself up and never keeps a record of wrongs, it always puts the other first, that beloved spouse, the one you have promised to love and cherish until death do part.

Love is everything! Oh my Lord, I have only just got it! I have studied the Song of Songs for years enjoying its spiritual message, the reality of who I am as the Bride of Christ, but I am also an earthly bride, a woman with a body, a woman who needs love just as much in the practical bedroom as in the heavenly bedroom.

The NO ENTRY signs have been removed, Holy Spirit has done His work, creativity is flowing in ways I would never have believed but the best is kept until last! The love of a man for a woman, the love of a woman for a man, the beauty of that original creation stolen from us by the serpent. We have all eaten from the tree of the knowledge of good and evil, but God is taking everyone who wants this, back to the garden of Eden, back to the paradise of unashamed nakedness back to taste the original fruit, the taste of plums!

The cherubim, the winged creatures who guard the way to the Tree of Life have stepped aside, the flaming sword turns into Jesus, the Word made flesh. The Holy Dove emerges from my womb singing its song, welcoming me as His new creation.

The vision melts away and in walks the love of my life, my husband, the father of my children. He has tears in his eyes as he reaches out towards me, enfolding me in his embrace. We do not need to say anything, for we have both been touched, we have both been transformed, transformed by the Creator's love.

"It is time to eat some plums!" I say watching the surprise on his face turn into delight as I start to remove our clothes.

CHAPTER 19
A CORD OF THREE STRANDS

I am back in the rose garden with Jesus.

"Are you enjoying your second honeymoon?" He asks, His eyes twinkling brightly.

"Oh yes!" I say happily "I never knew it could be this lovely. How clever of you to invent all this!"

"Well, I can't take all the credit, Abba and Holy Spirit also contributed. Creation in its purest form always comes in three parts." He continues.

I don't understand.
   "Come with Me," He says guiding me into the little garden shed in the corner of the garden, nestled against the wall. He reaches for a piece of rope and begins to tie it into a knot consisting of three strands or cords.

He begins to show me that two of the cords represent myself and my husband and the third cord is Himself. He explains that in order for this cord to remain unbroken, all three pieces must be in communion with one another. Each of us must enjoy an intimate

relationship with one another for the full beauty of this most holy of communions to be released. That is
Intimacy between the husband and God
Intimacy between the wife and God
Intimacy between the husband and wife.

When any of these parts is missing then the cord will be easily broken.

The world has bought into the lie, the counterfeit, the lust that excites for a short time and then leaves us empty, more empty that we have ever felt before.

Unfortunately, once you have become one with another person, you will inherit all their stuff, the good and the bad. You will become more and more emotionally disturbed and need deeper healing than ever. It is a merry-go-round into oblivion.

I remember the relationships before my husband, the ache in my heart, my low self-esteem. How I turned to men to make me feel better and to find love, but instead it led me further and further into despair and rejection. I, like many other women since the beginning of time, have used seductive charms to get what I want because I was not loved properly. None of us can love properly until we have been wooed by the greatest Lover of all time. We are all a bit of a mess really!

I realise with a jolt that so often I have over reacted to something my husband has said. There was an unhealed wound in my soul that was made before I even met him. It was a wound of deep rejection, and I saw rejection where there was none.

"You, My precious bride, have been given the greatest gift of all, a husband who has loved you from the very beginning, a husband who has loved you in the best way he was capable of at the time, a husband who has provided for you and has been your anchor. A husband who has remained faithful to you even when he didn't understand you at all."

He hands me the knot and for some inexplicable reason a picture of myself as a baby comes to my mind. I have just been born and the umbilical cord has yet to be cut to separate me from my mother. My Father is embracing the two of us. A midwife appears and cuts the cord, the cord tying me to the mother church, and instead plugs me back into the original source, Mother God.

I can't breathe, I panic and then the supernatural peace envelops me pushing me deeper down into my belly. I am looking down on my body from above and I see a kiss planted on my belly by Jesus. This kiss begins its journey upwards soaring out of my mouth as new life, new breath. I feel the deep freedom as I begin to breathe from my belly for the very first time. I will be able to sing properly now, I think, I will no longer get short of breath before the sentence is finished.

I begin to sing:

"Let your fingers, Jesus, move over the strings of my heart, let the music begin
Let the sound soar through the air catching the birds as they fly overhead.

Let their voices join in with the music being released
inside me
Together let our symphony rise up to Your ears
Let all Your creation worship alongside us
Calling for You, Jesus
Calling for You to return
Calling for You to come and set up Your kingdom here
on earth
Coming as the Heavenly Bridegroom, the Lion of Judah,
King of Kings, Lord of Lords.

Come, Lord Jesus, come soon
Come and save your creation
We are all groaning in frustration
Awaiting your physical presence
Believing by faith that you will come and topple the
Ruling spirits and principalities.
Prepare us, Your brides, Jesus
As we wait for Your return
Let the sound soar heavenwards
The sound of our hearts calling for
The Lover of our souls.
Spirit to spirit
Reaching upwards into the heavens
Reaching, grasping every drop of You
We can devour.
Drip feed us with Your Spirit
Ever increasing, filling our arteries and veins
Filling our hearts and minds with the Essence of You.

A Spirit of Jesus transfusion right into our bloodstreams
Jesus, Jesus, more of You,
Jesus, Jesus, more of Your touch

Your love, Your presence.
Let us reach out and put our hands in Yours
Let our fingers probe deeply into the pierced wounds in
Your hands
Let the current, the power which is in these wounds
Fill us as we touch and feel Your pain
Let Your love and compassion for Your creation
Flood into our hearts
Never to be the same again
Never to be hard again
A softness is coming, a heart full of flesh
So full of Jesus, so full of love
Come, Lord Jesus, come
Fill our hearts
Let our lights be shining brightly
Let us sing our new song
Let us dance our new dance
As we rush out to meet our Bridegroom
Here, He comes
He comes with His heavenly chariot
He comes with a multitude of angels
He comes with the trumpet fanfare
He comes to take His place upon the throne
The throne of our hearts
He comes to claim His bride.

Behold, He comes riding in the clouds
His destination, mount Zion
Behold, He comes drawing His bride from near and far
Behold, He comes to rule and reign from Zion
To disperse the enemy with a love that knocks them
flying
A love which brings men to their knees

A love which the devil cannot control, cannot manipulate,
cannot conquer
A love full of sacrifice and pain
A love as strong as death
A love burning as a furnace
A love that can never be quenched
A love that saves the lost
A love that welcomes the broken
A love that releases the oppressed
Love which transcends all
LOVE, what is LOVE?
It is JESUS, It is HIM
He is all in all
He is past, present, future
HE IS. HE IS LOVE."

CHAPTER 20
RECONCILIATION

I am sitting on the red sofa in heaven between Papa God and Jesus. Simultaneously they begin to speak, the harmony of their union echoes deep within me as Holy Spirit adds His voice.

"Come let Us write together
Write together of the One we love
The bride of Christ, how We love her
The bride of Messiah, how We long to know her
To be a part of her every day.

As We sit together in the heavenly places
As We look down together over the earth

We see a toxic cloud covering most of Our bride, Our church
This toxic cloud has become thicker and thicker
Over the centuries
Thick with the heresies
Thick with the reasoning and so called special knowledge
Thick with deception, religiosity, witchcraft.

As We sit looking down over this earth
This earth that We have made

Our hearts are stirred
Stirred by the intercessors
Stirred by the prayers of the saints over the generations
The scales are about to be tipped
For the incense has tipped the bowl over
Over to overflowing.
We feel the release inside Us as the sobs begin
Great sobs coming up from the depths of Our Beings.

The tears begin to fall, slowly at first
Gently piercing the cloud
Then the pressure builds as the torrents fall to the earth
Pent up emotion, pent up love and compassion
Released at last
Dissolving the deception
Removing the toxic power
The seducing power to which our people were held sway
But no! This is not the way!
This is the counterfeit
This is satan's territory.

The storm has begun
The storm to sweep in the end times
It cannot be held back any longer
The storm will bring clarity at last
But also the heartache that will go with it.
It is time, Beloved, to ride in the storm with Us
It is time to trust and rest with Us
The boat is approaching the top of the waterfall.
The boat is about to plunge down
Down through the roaring water
Down and down, over the rocks
The boat is knocked

The boat is torn
The boat carries on regardless.

We watch from the balconies of heaven
We watch as the church is brought to its knees
We watch as the world leaders and governments
Are changed
We watch as Our people infiltrate every mountain,
Every influential position
Babylon has had its day.

We watch the media giants stumble
We watch the disarray
We watch the rubble and the burning
We turn our faces away
Echoes of the cross call out as we watch
The horror take its course.
The earth begins to rumble
The dead begin to mobilise
The army is coming together
Limb by limb
Organ by organ
The army begins to awaken
They move together as one

Collecting every tribe and nation
Brother and sister
Father and mother
The Body is assembling
All coming into their rightful place."

As the smoke drifts up from the debris
We know the time is right

I smile, and My Father nods
"It is time, My Son
Time to take Your place
Time for the Head to return to its Body
Time for the Bridegroom to collect His bride."

CHAPTER 21
THE BIGGER PICTURE

The moon shines brightly and the stars twinkle gloriously in the night sky. All is dark, all is still and calm. But is it?

A rumbling is beginning, nature is fighting back.

Fighting back against the turmoil and pain.

Darkness covers the earth here, but on the other side of the world, the sun is shining brightly. People are going about their business, taking trains, buying sandwiches, wearing smart suits and reading newspapers as the commuter traffic begins to build. Stress levels escalate as people are encouraged to hurry, to work later, come in earlier. Working is all that matters, family life is discouraged. It is relentless, this life in the world, like a hamster on a wheel, it seems impossible to get off, or does it?

What is happening in the home? Children left in care, mothers encouraged to work, part time, full time, it matters not. For the woman's work is never done, they say. They work well into the night, sorting laundry, making packed lunches, ironing, cleaning...

Will it never end?

The darkness has engulfed all this land, whether momentarily in the day or the night. The enemy has encroached, people seem unable to rest, unwilling to just be, unwilling to enjoy the moment in case they are labelled lazy.

People pleasing, people pleasing, better schools, better houses, better holidays.
We must keep up with the Jones's, we must be better, more successful!
But what, I ask, does it mean to be successful?
What does it mean to have it all?

The earth is rumbling, the quake is close, people seem oblivious, lost in petty squabbles or lost inside a screen. A virtual world has taken over, cyber bullying and cybersex, they are the order of the day.
But night is approaching, moving steadily onwards, the light is receding and moving out of the way.

The earth opens up, the screaming begins.
The earth begins to swallow mankind
The volcano erupts, its molten lava running down the mountains
Burning, scorching everything in its way.

A light is seen in the sky
It is getting brighter, nearer.
A figure dressed in white
A figure who seems to be the Light
Is riding on the clouds.
Terror grips the people
"We thought we had more time," they scream.
"We thought we had more time."
The dawning of the truth upon the hearts of men

Men rebellious to the last
And now it is too late to change.
Or is it?

This poem lights the way.

The way to the truth
The truth is Jesus, Son of God
The carpenter from Nazareth.
He is the Jewish Messiah
A Saviour born in Israel
A nation, a land chosen
The apple of His eye.

He came, this Jesus, to save the lost
He came, this Jesus, that none should perish
He came to give mankind a second chance
He came to take our punishment
He died on the cross for you and me
He came to set us free
Free from the darkness that brings unbelief
Free from death and hell.

Rewind, rewind, you plead
Let us start again
Give us another chance
Just one more, please, just one more.

The bell rings on and on in my head.
Where am I? Where am I?
Clarity comes slowly, I am still in bed.
It was only a dream, well a nightmare really.
Or was it?
This is your wake up call, Beloved,

This is your second chance.
Repent and turn from your evil ways
And turn at last to Jesus
Turn to the one who loves you most
Who is waiting, yearning and praying for you.

For yes, despite all your rebellion and unbelief
He loves you anyway
He loves you so much that He died to set you free.
Take His hand, this gift of life and love
And step into a new world
A life of relationship and eternal life.
He's waiting here for you.

CHAPTER 22
ROYAL DESTINY

Jesus is waiting for me just inside the door to our secret garden. I jump in fright at the suddenness of His appearing.

"Why were you so close to the door?" I ask.

"I have been waiting. Come with Me."

I am surprised at the seriousness of His tone and also that He seems to be in a hurry. This is most unlike Jesus, He normally acts as if He has all the time in the world.

He takes me towards a door that has mysteriously appeared in the far wall, it is a rather grand double door with gold handles. Two angels are stationed either side of the doors and, as we approach, they are opened in front of us.

We seem to be in a huge library full of books. I have never seen such an enormous room in my life and the shelves seem to go on and on. Jesus grabs my hand and takes me down one of the rows and comes to a stop in front of a step ladder. He climbs up the ladder and reaches up to one of the shelves and then picks up a large brown leather book and brings it down so that I can see. I am surprised to see my name emblazoned on the front in bright olive green.

"This is the book of your life, Beloved. This was written before the foundation of the world and in it is written the calling we have placed on you."

He looks at me seriously and continues.

"Everyone has a book in this library, everyone has been given a certain calling and gifts and talents in order to carry this destiny out. Every person on earth is equally important to Us, there is no one who is more anointed than any other, it all depends on the individual being willing to say yes. If they do, We will come and work in them and change them from the inside out. We will heal them, refine them, purify and sanctify them. Then they will be ready to step into the destiny waiting here for them. A destiny that will fit them exactly, a destiny that will be so very easy, a destiny that will be so successful that the victor's crown will be waiting for them in heaven.

Do not think that we have called you all into ministry, many are called into business to help fund the Kingdom of God on earth. Others are called to minister through the caring professions, others are called to bring up children who will go on to impact thousands of souls. We are very inventive and every calling is created personally for each one. Whatever calling you have been given, you will absolutely adore. No longer will you struggle in jobs you hate, no longer will you have to work all hours and still feel inadequate.

You will discover the importance of rest and when you follow Our divine pattern, when you learn to put Us first, followed by your spouses and families, your businesses and ministries will flourish. For as you delight yourselves in Us, We will give you the desires of your hearts.

It is time for the Body of Christ to come to Us and ask Us what their destiny is, it is time to reach up and grasp the reality that all We are interested in is having a relationship with each one of you. One day you will be called before the judgement seat to give an account of your life. You will not be judged on what you did, you will be judged on what you were called to do. This is why I have called you in here today, Beloved, for I want to show you your destiny."

He hands me a scroll but I already know what is written inside.

I am called to sing His Song of Love and join with Him to call His church to become His bride. Many are called to the wedding banquet but few enter in. Some come in as guests but He wants us all to be His bride and come into the fullness of our reward in His Kingdom.

He hands me another scroll, this is the scroll of remembrance, in here is written every word I have spoken honouring our Lord and every act of obedience.

"Those who appear in this scroll will be my jewels, my treasured possessions. I will honour them in eternity as they have honoured me on earth.

Go write a book in six days explaining everything I have shown you. On the seventh day you must take a Sabbath Rest, for this is My divine pattern and those who ignore it will ignore it at their peril."

He then hands me the blueprint for the book, the book that you now hold in your hands.

May we all come fully into our destiny and enjoy intimacy with our Lord here and now in this life.

When we enter into eternity with Him, may we be honoured as His precious bride and take our place at His side.

About the Author

Mandy Imlay has fallen in love with the Living God. She has been transformed by the Creator's Love and seen His supernatural power bring healing and reconciliation in every area of her life.

She and her husband, Andrew, are the founders of a new online ministry called Come Away with Me. It is a fusion of creative worship promoting unity and intimacy with Jesus. They have a desire to see Jews and Gentiles come together and see the miraculous outpouring of love and healing that would bring.

They live in Berkshire, England and have three grown up children.

website address: www.comeawaywithme.org

THE END

Lightning Source UK Ltd.
Milton Keynes UK
UKHW01f0440090618
323987UK00001B/53/P